Family Lawyer Marketing
MORE CLICKS · MORE CALLS · MORE CLIENTS

Family Attorney Guide To Landing More Clients

How Law Practices In The Google Maps Local 3-Pack Reel In Clients Month After Month on Auto-Pilot

By: Aaron T. Landreth
Owner, Family Lawyer Marketing

Are You Ready For More Clicks, More Calls and More Clients?
Visit to Schedule Your Call – www.FamilyLawyerMarketing.com

Family Lawyer Marketing

MORE CLICKS · MORE CALLS · MORE CLIENTS

© 2019 Family Lawyer Marketing. ALL RIGHTS RESERVED. No part of this book may be reproduced or transmitted in any form whatsoever, electronic, or mechanical, including photocopying, recording, or by any informational storage or retrieval system without the expressed written, dated and signed permission from the author.

LIMITS OF LIABILITY / DISCLAIMER OF WARRANTY:

The author and publisher of this book have used their best efforts in preparing this material. The author and publisher make no representation or warranties with respect to the accuracy, applicability, fitness, or completeness of the contents of this program. They disclaim any warranties (expressed or implied), merchantability, or fitness for any particular purpose. The author and publisher shall in no event be held liable for any loss or other damages, including but not limited to special, incidental, consequential, or other damages. As always, the advice of a competent legal, tax, accounting or other professional should be sought

Are You Ready For More Clicks, More Calls and More Clients?
Visit to Schedule Your Call – www.FamilyLawyerMarketing.com

Family Lawyer Marketing
MORE CLICKS · MORE CALLS · MORE CLIENTS

About the Author

Hi! Nice to meet you, my name is Aaron Landreth. I'm the author of this very book you are reading, so I thought it would be good to tell you a little bit about myself.

I started my marketing journey helping local businesses in 2010. I had already established a lead generating system for a mortgage company that took their agency from $0 in digital marketing revenue to over $150k in 9 months.

With that success firm in hand, I branched out and went solo. My client base rapidly grew, working with many companies across a broad spectrum of industries, including big names in Direct Marketing, Carpet Cleaning, Damage Restoration, CPA's, Attorneys, Dentists and Multi-Media Audio Visual companies to name a few. Annual digital marketing revenues grew to over $1M.

The opportunity to work with such a diverse range of industries allowed me to stay on top of digital marketing trends, what's working, what's not, and how to leverage the greatest results with each marketing dollar.

You may not believe it, but it's true – <u>You now have more opportunity to grow your practice and reach more people, with LESS Ad spend than ever before.</u>

My goal with this book is to translate my learnings into an easy to follow guide that will help your practice to increase visibility, get more clients, and ultimately earn more money.

Below, you have our email to request the TOP 50+ Directories for Family Law Firms and Solo Practices. It's an invaluable resource to jump start your visibility.

My wish is that you will take this information and prosper with clients reaching out to YOU, instead of the other way around.

If you would like assistance with any of the strategies outlined in this book, or help generating clients for your Family Law Practice, we are here to help. Our contact information is also located in the footer of every page.

Our strategies, which include online directory marketing combined with mass media exposure, video syndication, and Google My Business 3-Pack placement are strategies proven to generate more clients, over and over again.

To Your Success, Aaron Landreth

Family Lawyer Marketing

MORE CLICKS · MORE CALLS · MORE CLIENTS

Visit to Schedule Consultation
To Get More Click, Take More Calls and Win More Clients
https://www.familylawyermarketing.com

Email To Request Your Top 50+ Directory and
Citation Listings for Family Law Firms:

Top50@FamilyLawyerMarketing.com

Are You Ready For More Clicks, More Calls and More Clients?
Visit to Schedule Your Call – www.FamilyLawyerMarketing.com

Family Lawyer Marketing
MORE CLICKS · MORE CALLS · MORE CLIENTS

For Family Law Firms and Solo Practices, appearing in Google Maps Local 3-Pack is **THE** single most important thing you can do to increase phone calls, leads and customers as you will learn in this guide.

What is the '3-Pack' and Why Is It So Powerful?

The 3-Pack is a group of three local businesses that appear at the very top of Google search listings, or just below a section of paid advertisements.

The 3-Pack ranks in the #1 position in 93% of Google searches, according to a study by seoClarity (link: https://www.seoclarity.net/how-googles-local-pack-update-has-reshaped-the-organic-landscape-12952/).

This makes being seen prominently in the 3-Pack essential for your businesses.

The 3-Pack quickly reveals to searchers that you are the most trusted & relevant, especially when combined with the right review profile.

In other words, it provides an at-a-glance snapshot of your business in a busy world where **people area making buying decisions** based on:

a) whether they can find your business at all

b) what others are saying about you.

Key Takeaway: People are Making Buying Decisions When Seeing the 3-Pack in Search Results.

Being ranked highly in the 3 pack goes beyond just visibility or maps ranking for maps ranking sake. In fact, it directly ties into a buying decision.

Research by Google (link: https://www.thinkwithgoogle.com/marketing-resources/micro-moments/purchase-decision-mobile-growth/) shows that 76% of people who conduct a local search contact a business within 24 hours, and 28% of those searches result in a purchase of a service.

So, when you are ranked highly within the 3-Pack, you are on your way to more phone calls and increased sales of your services.

As shown below, the 3-Pack does a few things…

From their phone, customers can click on your business's name, which gives customers more information about your company, including a click-to-call button.

Or, customers can use a click-to-call button directly from the 3-Pack results.

Family Lawyer Marketing
MORE CLICKS · MORE CALLS · MORE CLIENTS

Click to call is essential to the growth of your business because a Google study (link: https://www.thinkwithgoogle.com/consumer-insights/click-to-call) shows that **70% of mobile searchers click-to-call a business from Google results**.

In a world of constant smart phone usage, your (customers, patients, clients) want a way to push a button and instantly be connected to your business.

Are You Ready For More Clicks, More Calls and More Clients?
Visit to Schedule Your Call – www.FamilyLawyerMarketing.com

Family Lawyer Marketing
MORE CLICKS · MORE CALLS · MORE CLIENTS

Since *3-Pack results are largely displayed based on the location of the searcher*, your ability to get more phone calls and leads to your business is based on two critical factors:

1) <u>Visibility.</u> You need to outrank your competitors and be seen in as many parts of town as possible, and there are many factors that play into your ability to achieve this; and

2) <u>Reviews</u> (and a lot of them) *Nothing will get a potential client to act faster than a lot of glowing reviews.* On the other hand, a lack of reviews or negative reviews can be damaging to your business.

Google Users Trust the Google 3-Pack More Than Paid Ads

There are a few ways to gain visibility on Page 1 of Google's local search results:

1) Pay for ads through Google AdWords
2) Be ranked highly in the 3-Pack
3) Be one of the top 10 organic listings below the 3-Pack.

Because your advertising budget is vital to the success of your business, you may be wondering *which section gets the most attention though*?

<u>The 3-Pack is the clear winner.</u>

Why?...

Are You Ready For More Clicks, More Calls and More Clients?
Visit to Schedule Your Call – www.FamilyLawyerMarketing.com

Family Lawyer Marketing
MORE CLICKS · MORE CALLS · MORE CLIENTS

The 3-Pack is consistently noticed more often when it comes to local searches.

Google ads fall behind both the 3-Pack and the top 10 organic results because people don't find paid ads to be trustworthy or relevant in search engine results.

A study by Search Engine Watch (link: https://searchenginewatch.com/sew/opinion/2423578/google-local-pack-is-233-percent-more-important) found that:

1) 68% of searchers prefer the local 3-Pack
2) 27 percent prefer the organic results below the 3-Pack
3) Only 10 percent trust paid search results.

As you can see, with the 3-Pack garnering 68% of all searcher's trust, high placement in the 3-Pack is an absolute must.

Family Lawyer Marketing
MORE CLICKS - MORE CALLS - MORE CLIENTS

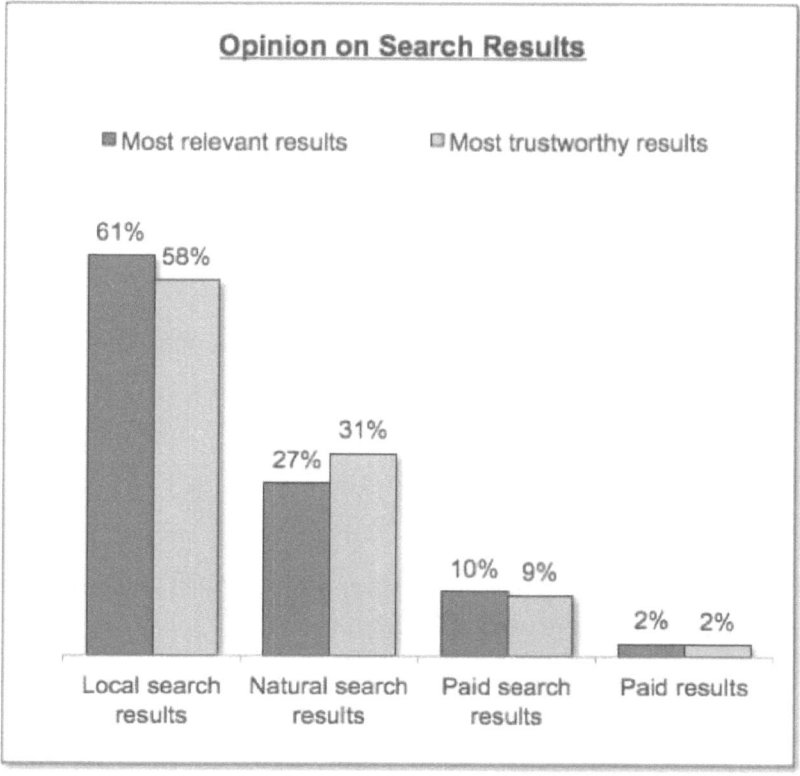

Also, paid search results often provide little return on investment because the average cost per click is very high and growing every year, with some popular keyword-clicks for Family Lawyers costing as much as $50-$100 or more. **_(OUCH!)_**

Are You Ready For More Clicks, More Calls and More Clients?
Visit to Schedule Your Call – www.FamilyLawyerMarketing.com

Family Lawyer Marketing
MORE CLICKS · MORE CALLS · MORE CLIENTS

In addition, companies that use AdWords see a very low click-through rate of 2% or less according to WordStream (link: https://www.wordstream.com/average-ctr).

Even if you manage to get a decent number of clicks, the average conversion is dismal at 2-3% on the high end.

That means you would need about 100 clicks to get just 2-3 phone calls.

Only 2-3 Phone calls per 100 Clicks is not very appealing, right?

You do it and I do too – We've Gone "Ad Blind"…

Google users skip paid ads and move straight to the 3-Pack to determine which business they should contact.

Will it be yours?

And if 2 % of all clicks and a 2-3% conversion rate doesn't sound appealing, how about 44%?

<u>The 3-Pack receives the majority of actual clicks on a results page, at a 44% rate</u>, according to Moz (link: https://moz.com/blog/the-new-snack-pack-where-users-clicking-how-you-can-win).

Are You Ready For More Clicks, More Calls and More Clients?
Visit to Schedule Your Call – www.FamilyLawyerMarketing.com

Family Lawyer Marketing
MORE CLICKS - MORE CALLS - MORE CLIENTS

The results are below.

	# of Clicks	Total Clicks
Paid Clicks	30	19%
Top 3 Local Clicks	69	44%
More Local Results Clicks	12	8%
Organic Clicks	45	29%
Total Clicks	156	

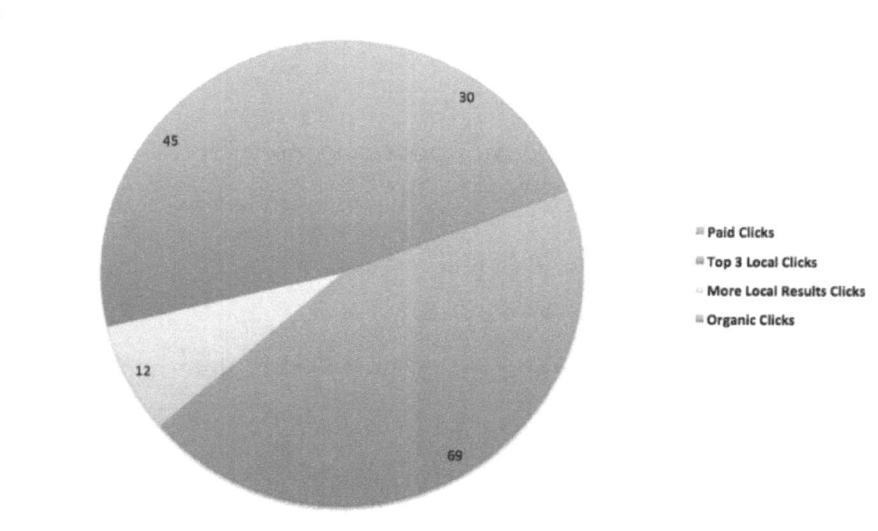

The Moz study shows that **searchers like the 3-Pack the most**.

The results also found that searchers were less likely to click on the business website link or directions.

Are You Ready For More Clicks, More Calls and More Clients?
Visit to Schedule Your Call – www.FamilyLawyerMarketing.com

Instead, they clicked on the business name itself, which sends customers to a Google My Business listing where they can find the business's phone number.

And recall from above, that *your potential clients make actual buying decisions from the 3 pack*.

It's important to note that businesses that did not have reviews received **no interest** at all from searchers (more on the importance of reviews below).

The study showed that positive reviews are vital to spark customer interest and are a must to be noticed within the 3-Pack.

Finally, this study along with the next one shows that companies with the highest rating in the 3-Pack received the most attention.

Though the organic listings in the second study represented 40% of the clicks and finished first, the 3-Pack finished second with 33% percent of customer interest.

See the heat map below.

Family Lawyer Marketing
MORE CLICKS · MORE CALLS · MORE CLIENTS

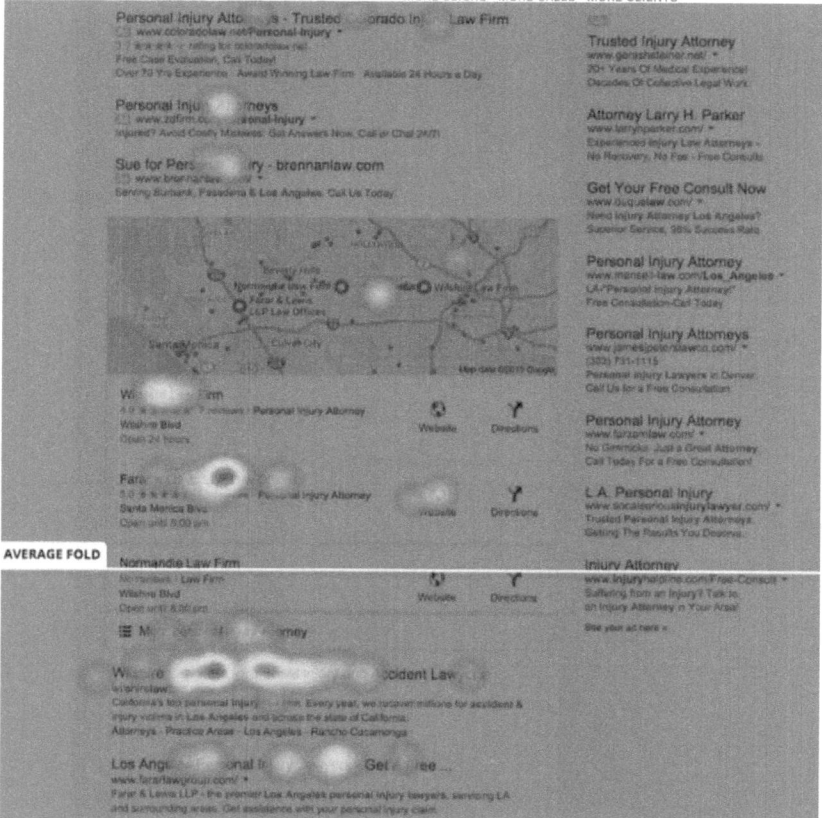

The first company in the 3-Pack is the same as the first company in the organic search results below it. The company received most of the attention likely because of its top spot in both categories.

Although, the second listing in the 3-Pack got a lot of attention as well because it has a 5-star status.

Are You Ready For More Clicks, More Calls and More Clients?
Visit to Schedule Your Call – www.FamilyLawyerMarketing.com

Family Lawyer Marketing
MORE CLICKS - MORE CALLS - MORE CLIENTS

The two top companies in the 3-pack received most of the attention on the page, and the business with no reviews did not receive any interest at all.

Again, it is worth pointing out that the 3-Pack clicks land on the business name itself, where users can find the company's phone number.

So while organic received a few more clicks in this study, it is likely that less phone calls resulted from those clicks.

Why?

Your potential clients place a huge emphasis on third party reviews, which typically don't appear on a website and when they do are less trustworthy.

Furthermore, after reading reviews, your potential clients are visiting your website less and less, and instead making their decision based on those reviews (see the Bright Local study later in this report).

Family Lawyer Marketing
MORE CLICKS · MORE CALLS · MORE CLIENTS

	# of Clicks	Total Clicks
Paid Clicks	12	13%
Top 3 Local Clicks	31	33%
More Local Results Clicks	13	14%
Organic Clicks	38	40%
Total Clicks	94	

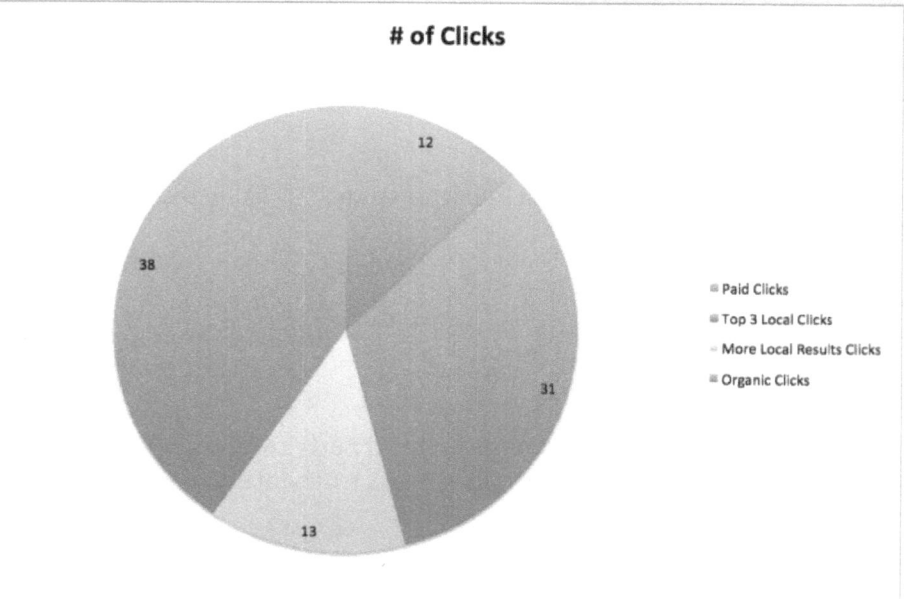

The Importance of Reviews on Your Google 3-Pack Listing

Customer reviews have a big impact on the behavior of customers and the performance of a company's brand.

Are You Ready For More Clicks, More Calls and More Clients?
Visit to Schedule Your Call – www.FamilyLawyerMarketing.com

Family Lawyer Marketing
MORE CLICKS · MORE CALLS · MORE CLIENTS

Reviews may quite literally make or break sales of services, and the quality and quantity of online feedback plays a huge role in a company's bottom line.

According to a survey by BrightLocal (link: https://www.brightlocal.com/learn/local-consumer-review-survey), 88% of consumers read online reviews, and 85% of people trust them just as much as a personal recommendation.

Importantly, a lack of user reviews on Google and other crowd-sourced review websites like Yelp, or ignoring consumer reviews as a potential marketing opportunity means that a company is excluding a whopping 88% of the buying community.

In other words, _consumers want to read reviews to help them with their buying decisions, and your business loses an opportunity to attract customers when they are deprived of them_.

While location and price can be important factors in choosing a local business, _no other factor is more important than positive customer reviews._

Research shows that 68% of customers are more likely to use a local business after reading positive reviews, while **40% of customers go to competitors when they read bad reviews.**

Are You Ready For More Clicks, More Calls and More Clients?
Visit to Schedule Your Call – www.FamilyLawyerMarketing.com

Family Lawyer Marketing
MORE CLICKS · MORE CALLS · MORE CLIENTS

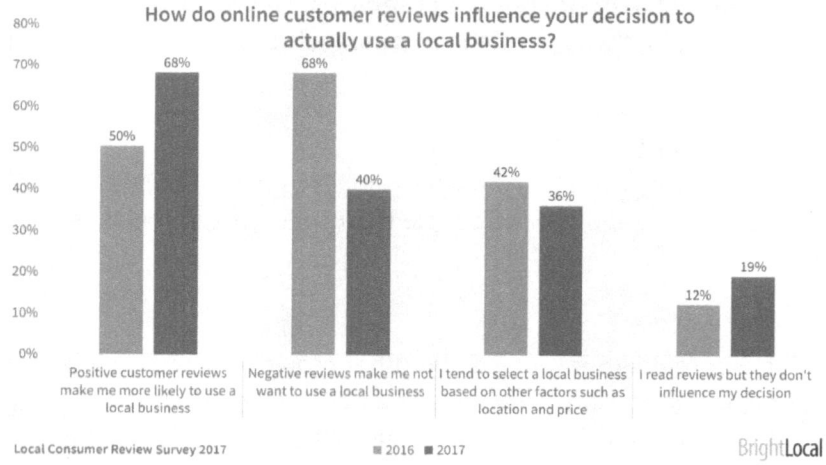

Local Consumer Review Survey 2017 — 2016 ■ 2017 — BrightLocal

More Stars Equals More Clicks on Your Google Maps 3-Pack

The average number of stars that a company receives makes a huge impression on customers and influences the rate at which they contact a company in the 3-Pack.

Listings with five-star reviews earned 69% of the attention on the 3-Pack, while four stars earned 59% of the attention, and three stars earned 44%.

Are You Ready For More Clicks, More Calls and More Clients?
Visit to Schedule Your Call – www.FamilyLawyerMarketing.com

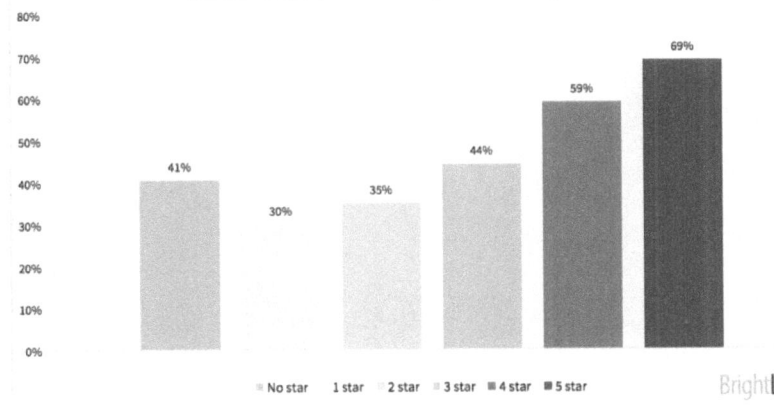

Also, the number of reviews is important for consumer trust. *Customers read as many as 21 or more reviews before making a purchase of services.*

The normal range is between 2 and 10 reviews, making up 83% of consumer needs, but 7% read 11-20 reviews, and 6% want feedback that exceeds 20 reviews.

So, **businesses that have less than 11 online reviews are missing an opportunity** to get the attention of 13 percent of the buying population. That is huge.

Are You Ready For More Clicks, More Calls and More Clients?
Visit to Schedule Your Call – www.FamilyLawyerMarketing.com

The Importance of Reviews on Google 3-Pack Visibility

Online reviews are also important because they can somewhat influence a business's ability to rank in the Google 3-Pack as well as in the organic or natural search engine results.

There is also some speculation that reviews on other third-party review sites can help you rank better as well.

According to *Forbes* (link: https://www.forbes.com/sites/jaysondemers/2015/12/28/how-important-are-customer-reviews-for-online-marketing/2/#690892d66027), Google uses information from many third-party directories and review sites, such as Yelp.

Whether Google only factors in Google reviews or third-party reviews as well, the bottom line is that the more positive reviews you have, the higher your chance becomes at ranking in Google's 3-Pack, and not below the 3-Pack line, where you will find a link to "More places."

You do not want to be in this spot because you completely lose visibility.

The buying public simply doesn't look beyond the 3 pack.

While ranking in local organic search results (the results that appear just below the 3 pack) continues to be a top factor in whether a company will rank in the 3 pack (typically depending on many variables not discussed here), a well optimized website and reviews dominated all other factors, according to Local SEO Guide (link: http://www.localseoguide.com/guides/local-seo-ranking-factors).

Why do reviews help?

Reviews help Google to use a number of signals for its ranking factors, and reviews help Google's search engine to determine trending businesses, which can increase a company's ranking.

This works because reviews have date stamps, so current customer engagement is visible to the engine.

That is why you will observe in the graph below that average weekly and monthly reviews, as well as new reviews in the past
month, play a big role in the search results placement within a 3-Pack.

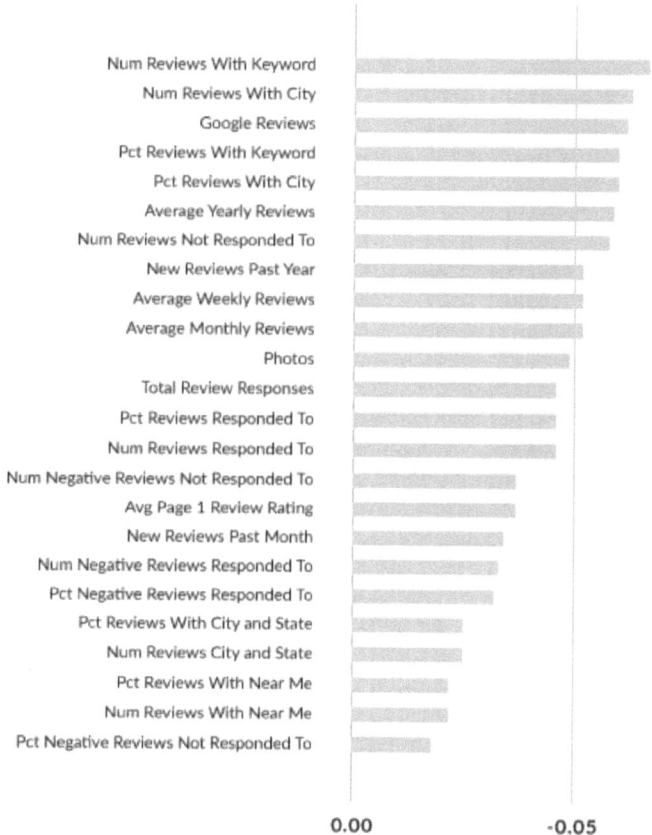

The bottom line on reviews? The importance of online reviews is rising in every important customer category, and numerous surveys indicate that consumers want reviews when making a buying decision.

Are You Ready For More Clicks, More Calls and More Clients?
Visit to Schedule Your Call – www.FamilyLawyerMarketing.com

Also, Google's search results use consumer reviews when determining rankings factors for the 3-Pack.

User reviews are important, and that will not change. So, *the longer you wait to start optimizing your reviews, the more you stand to lose.*

Online shoppers demand reviews and they are responsible for better online visibility and ranking in organic search results and within the 3-Pack.

Websites Are Becoming Less Of A Factor.

A Bright Local study conducted for the past several years shows a trend that simply can't be ignored.

Consumers are relying less and less on websites to determine if they will do business with you or not.

Instead, what matters is what is discussed in this report. Visibility (appearing in the 3 pack for as many keywords as possible in as many parts of town as possible) and reviews.

Bright Local concluded the following:

Key Findings

Family Lawyer Marketing
MORE CLICKS · MORE CALLS · MORE CLIENTS

- 17% fewer people will visit a business website after reading good reviews than in 2016 (37% this year compared to 54% in 2016)
- The number of consumers who would visit a business as their next step has grown by 10% in the last year to 17%
- 10% of consumers now contact a business after reading a positive review

Link: https://www.brightlocal.com/learn/local-consumer-review-survey/

What does this mean for you?

You must start to work with digital marketing companies whose top priority is to understand that consumers are visiting websites less every year and instead are relying on visibility and a solid review profile to determine if they call you, or come in to your place of business at all.

It's that important. Unfortunately, most digital marketing companies are only focused on ranking websites in the organic search engine results or managing an Adwords campaign.

None of these have the trust, visibility and attention of your potential customer like the 3 pack does.

Conclusion

Appearing in the Google Maps Local 3-Pack is the first step to attracting attention to your law practice and encouraging people to call your business.

Family Lawyer Marketing

MORE CLICKS · MORE CALLS · MORE CLIENTS

Work to create a superior Google 3 pack presence and look sharp and relevant with lots of positive reviews or suffer defeat at the hands of perceptive business owners who compete with you and are already heavily leveraging these factors.

Visit to Schedule Consultation
To Get More Click, Take More Calls and Win More Clients
https://www.familylawyermarketing.com

Email To Request Your Top 50+ Directory and
Citation Listings for Family Law Firms:

Top50@FamilyLawyerMarketing.com

Are You Ready For More Clicks, More Calls and More Clients?
Visit to Schedule Your Call – www.FamilyLawyerMarketing.com

www.ingramcontent.com/pod-product-compliance
Lightning Source LLC
Chambersburg PA
CBHW031511210526
45463CB00008B/3193